WALL ART

WALL ART

Megamurals & Supergraphics

Photographs by Stefan Merken
Text by Betty Merken

RUNNING PRESS
Philadelphia, Pennsylvania

To Aaron

Canadian representatives: General Publishing Co., Ltd., 30 Lesmill Road, Don Mills,
Ontario M3B 2T6.
International representatives: Worldwide Media Services, Inc., 115 East 23rd Street,
New York, NY 10010.

9 8 7 6 5 4 3 2 1
Digit on the right indicates the number of this printing.

Library of Congress Cataloging-in-Publication Data
Merken, Stefan.
    Wall art.

    Includes index.
    1. Street art — California — Themes, motives. 2. Mural painting and decoration —
20th century — California — Themes, motives. 3. Mural painting and decoration,
American — California — Themes, motives. I. Merken, Betty. II. Title.
ND2635. CaM47 1987   751.7'3'09794   87-16433
ISBN 0-89471-572-0.

Printed by Leefung-Asco Printers Ltd., Hong Kong
Cover Design by Toby Schmidt
Typography: Gill Sans Bold Condensed and Gill Sans Medium by Precision Graphics,
Pennsauken, New Jersey

This book may be ordered by mail from the publisher. Please include $1.50 postage.
But try your bookstore first! Running Press Book Publishers, 125 South 22nd Street,
Philadelphia, PA 19103.

CONTENTS

Imagine yourself in Los Angeles on a warm, clear Sunday morning. Driving along Ocean Park Boulevard toward the beach, you glance to the right, and there alongside you looms a fantastic painted image nearly a block long: a brilliant and stunning fantasy, it portrays a dozen or more carousel horses unbridling themselves and breaking away from the landmark Santa Monica Pier Carousel, galloping and prancing with delicious abandon toward the sea.

This enormous mural, in so public a place, allows you to enter the imaginary world of the artist, to identify with the spirited horses, and to experience multiple levels of fantasy and metaphor — all this on an ordinary public wall, accessible to anyone by car or on foot (see page 80).

Closer to the beach, a turn into a sleepy little alley in Venice brings you face-to-face with a modest garage door (see page 38). Painted there is a dreamy, surreal image of an old woman walking on the beach, pulling her groceries behind her. On a distant horizon behind her, three bathing beauties of the 1930s, lucid reminders of her youth, beckon with waving arms and beguiling smiles. In the foreground, an obtuse young woman in shorts glides by on roller skates, oblivious to all around her, as if this beach is and always was her domain. The provocative effect of this mural deepens when you see, painted near the bottom, a fragment of a newspaper article headlining the forced removal of senior citizens from their cherished apartments.

Murals as compelling as these appear and disappear all over Los Angeles — on walls, on garage doors, in alleys, in the barrios, on the freeways. Although you will find these murals in almost every town in California, Los Angeles always has had the greatest number. It is estimated that today Los Angeles has as many as 5,000 outdoor murals, making it the model city for mural art.

Perhaps the openness and freedom of expression that characterize the lifestyle of Southern California help to make Los Angeles, with its omnipresent sunshine, a fertile place for public art. In exchange for this openness and freedom of expression, however, mural artists must undergo working conditions that would dishearten most of us — turbulent freeways, traffic congestion, and automobile pollution — and the murals themselves are often victimized by vigilante graffiti and defacement.

Some of these murals are painted almost overnight; many others are the culmination of months of planning, organizing, and fundraising. All require strenuous physical labor. However accomplished, these murals transcend mere decoration: for as they embellish our urban environment, they also affect our perception, our aesthetic, and our politics, and in many cases they educate us as well.

"Millions crowd the freeways daily, and murals might be the only art they have ever seen," says Ruth Bachofner of the Ruth Bachofner Gallery in Los Angeles. "To some, the murals will stir or awaken curiosity and may open the avenue to museums and galleries."

The sheer number of public murals in Los Angeles is staggering; throughout the city, large painted images of every description loom up and catch your eye from the freeways and side streets, giving onramps new meaning and beckoning drivers to explore new and unknown neighborhoods.

The barrios and neighborhoods of East and Southeast Los Angeles are well worth this exploration. Mural art as a vehicle for social commentary is highly developed here, where Chicano artists shut out by establishment art galleries have taken their work to the public walls and with enormous pride and energy have created big art — immense, flamboyant images, born of a defiant social consciousness and nurtured by intense community pride. Many of these murals, painted well over a decade ago (and often inspired by early twentieth-century

Mexican muralists José Orozco, Diego Rivera, and David Alfaro Siqueiros) have been painted over and no longer exist. Scholars from around the world are attempting to locate information about the murals that have been destroyed and are amassing slides and information to document those that remain.

Chicano mural art proliferated in Los Angeles in the early 1970s, when talented artists portrayed the social realities of their neighborhoods and the conditions of their lives, and often tried to suggest alternatives. Many of these early Chicano muralists now have international reputations.

Two independent muralists, Wayne Healy and David Botello, began to work together on murals in 1975, calling themselves the Los Dos Streetscapers. Their work can be seen at the Estrada Courts and Ramona Gardens housing projects in Los Angeles, as well as at various other locations in Los Angeles (see pages 34 and 115). Art Alaniz and Rudy Calderon joined the Los Dos Streetscapers in 1980, and the group collectively became the East Los Streetscapers, a self-supporting artists' cooperative. The four artists continue to collaborate as muralists while also working independently to express their individual aesthetic visions. East Los Streetscaper murals such as *El Corrido de Boyle Heights* and *La Familia* (See pages 14 and 91) have received international exposure in publications and traveling exhibitions.

The civil rights movement of the 1960s and the social upheavals that followed sent artists searching for meaningful ways to link their politics to their creative expression. Despite the social activism of the 1960s and the 1970s, the art world, ironically, did little to address the social realities of many people's lives. So the emergence of mural art at that time seemed to be welcome fare for the insatiable appetites of many artists, minority and otherwise, who were barred from the mainstream of gallery art. For these artists, mural art could serve the multiple functions of validating their individual artistic identities, expressing the heritage and experience of their people, and portraying social and economic realities. Mural art also involved inner-city youth in creative work and served the cosmetic function of urban renewal and the beautification of communities.

The city of Chicago, with its strong tradition of labor protest and socially conscious art and literature, leads other American cities in its representation of murals from black communities. However, in Los Angeles, the neighborhoods near Watts and along Crenshaw Boulevard contain an abundance of murals expressing black heritage and values. Mural artist Alonzo Davis, a committed social activist, was instrumental in developing mural art in this part of the city (see pages 47 and 69) as well as in establishing the Brockman Gallery in Los Angeles to showcase the work of minority artists.

As artists continued to create on city walls, community organizations and municipal administrators began to recognize the importance of murals and to fund their production. The City Wide Mural Project was established in Los Angeles in 1974 with direct funding from the Los Angeles City Council to plan and execute community murals in diverse neighborhoods. Under the guidance of local mural artist Judy Baca, the City Wide Mural Project thrived. Later, from 1977 to 1983, artist Glenna Boltuch Avila directed the program, and under her enlightened direction the City Wide Mural Project provided Los Angeles communities with hundreds of murals painted in styles varying from figurative to expressionist. Many accomplished mural artists who are now working independently got their start through the City Wide Mural Project.

One such artist is Richard Wyatt, who has dedicated six years of his career to creating public imagery throughout the city of Los Angeles. "Most of these murals have been produced in communities which are generally under-served by the arts, especially the visual arts, due to the scarcity of museums and galleries in the immediate area," Wyatt says. "The subject matter in my work celebrates the multicultural sensibilities of L.A.'s diverse ethnic groups."

Beginning in the late 1960s, larger-than-life images, meant to engulf one's senses and to alter perceptions of reality, began appearing in Venice Beach in Southern California. Venice Beach, where one can expect to see anything, seemed just the place to provide the kind of artistic license necessary for the emergence of these types of murals. Here the images seem especially appropriate, even indigenous, and it is difficult now to imagine this beach community without them.

Two young artists, Terry Schoonhoven and Vic Henderson, were creating murals in Venice that were an extraordinary blending of superrealism and *trompe l'oeil*, with surrealistic overtones. Each artist had been working independently on realistic paintings tinged with surrealism, and had been disappointed with the gallery scene of the late 1960s. Their first collaborative effort was *Brooks Street Painting*, a mural on the outside wall of Vic Henderson's rented studio building in Venice, painted with the landlord's permission. The mural seemed to reflect the view from Schoonhoven's studio down the street, and was such a successful *trompe l'oeil* image that it caught the eye of many passers-by, including two other artists, Leonard Koren and Jim Frazen. Koren and Frazen joined the other two and became known collectively as the Los Angeles Fine Arts Squad. Together, they were instrumental in negotiating a mural commission for the Paris Biennale in 1971.

Another highly successful and immensely popular early mural commission of the Los Angeles Fine Arts Squad was *The Isle of California* (see page 27), completed in 1972. An image of ironic wit, it is a surrealistic forecast of a disastrous earthquake that sends California floating out into the Pacific Ocean. The year before, the Los Angeles Fine Arts Squad created a mural called *Venice in the Snow*, which was to become a landmark in Venice, California. With incredible realism, it depicted the beach community and its well-known local characters, all covered in snow — something that never happens in Southern California. Now obscured by an apartment house built inches away, *Venice in the Snow* is still a local landmark to community residents who peek sideways between the two buildings to see it.

Another surrealist mural artist is John Wehrle, famous for his 1976 mural on the De Young Museum in San Francisco which depicts the city and the freeway overtaken by wild animals, including some endangered species. Wehrle also graced Venice, California, with his own version of *The Fall of Icarus* (see page 92). This mural shows a drive-in theater overgrown with weeds; on the screen is an image of a floating astronaut, simultaneously witnessed by a cowboy on horseback and an angel in the back of a pickup truck.

For these early murals, longevity was not an issue. The paintings were treated as performances and were allowed to disintegrate. The early murals of Venice have faded dramatically, and now artists are using a silicate-based paint that is much more durable than the quick-drying enamels used in the late 1960s and early 1970s. Although the colors in the early murals of Venice have faded to shadows of their original intensity, the enigmatic and surrealistic images, with their juxtaposed reality, still suggest an investigation of the notions of time and place which is unique and enduring.

Terry Schoonhoven's most recent work, *City Scape* (see page 46), is a contemporary skyline which includes references to classical architecture, and can be seen in downtown in Los Angeles from the Sixth Street Overpass of the Harbor Freeway. Schoonhoven picked the site for pedestrian viewing, and the mural can be seen easily as you walk along Sixth Street toward the freeway.

John Wehrle's most recent mural, *Galileo, Apollo, Jupiter* (see page 74), which can be seen in downtown Los Angeles on the Hollywood Freeway between Broadway and Spring Streets, depicts a classical Greek temple orbiting Jupiter.

"Wall painting is the oldest of the arts," says Wehrle. "It's really only a short step from the caves of Lascaux to the freeways of Los Angeles.

"I like working with an art that lives where it's created. Each location has its own character, its own problems, its unique audience. I like doing paintings so large that they engage the periphery of vision, the primitive part of the eye that bypasses the cerebral cortex. Think of them as scenes from an epic film that the viewer completes in his mind. The painting provides the clues — you solve the mystery."

Another young visionary muralist, Kent Twitchell, began painting photorealistic portraits on a grand and magnificent scale on huge exterior walls in Los Angeles in the early 1970s. His *The Freeway Lady* (see page 62), a portrait of television actress Lillian Bronson, is located just off the Hollywood Freeway near Alvarado Street as you travel north. The most popular of Twitchell's murals, it was painted as a monument to the elderly. Twitchell researched books of faces at the Screen Actor's Guild in Los Angeles, looking for an image to resemble one of his two great-grandmothers. Lillian Bronson resembled both. After spending a month with photographs and layouts and sketching the mural, Twitchell spent two months painting the image, using acrylic paints which dried fast and held up beautifully.

The Freeway Lady was completed in 1974 and became a famous guardian of freeway travelers. But construction of a new motel in 1981 partially obscured the mural, allowing only the top half to remain visible. Then, late in 1986, a San Francisco-based sign company persuaded the owner of the building to allow an advertisement to be placed over the mural. *The Freeway Lady* was whited out early one Sunday morning and overpainted with the words "Your Ad Here" and a phone number. So many people called to complain that the phone had to be disconnected. What followed was the emergence of The Los Angeles Mural Conservancy, an organization founded by citizens and arts groups throughout the city to preserve and maintain Los Angeles murals — an art form that is precious, unique, and indigenous to Los Angeles. *The Freeway Lady* is currently being restored.

Kent Twitchell's immense portraits have a slightly surreal quality, perhaps due to the suggestive familiarity of the faces he chooses. It is well known that the commonest things become strangely uncommon when removed from their normal context, and it is in part because of this that Twitchell's work is so dramatic. Twitchell's *The Holy Trinity with the Virgin* (see page 118), which can be seen on the west wall of the main building at the Otis Art Institute of Parsons School of Design in Los Angeles, portrays TV series heroes as contemporary versions of Christ, the Virgin Mary, and God.

"I had been doing underground religious art," Twitchell says, "and I decided to paint an even more overt item on the west wall of the Institute. It was inspired by Massaccio's *Holy Trinity with the Virgin and Saint John*, a 15th-century altarpiece we studied in class. I dropped St. John and used local models whose presence would add meaning to the title. Jan Clayton posed as the Virgin. She was the Emmy Award-winning mother on TV's 'Lassie' in the mid-1950s.

"For Christ I asked Billy Gray to pose. He played the small son in the science fiction classic *The Day the Earth Stood Still*, and *Jim Thorp* as a boy. But mostly he starred in the acclaimed 'Father Knows Best' during his teens in the 1950s and 1960s . . . Billy was the ideal model for Jesus, being the son of the Father who knows best.

"For God the Father, Los Angeles had only one citizen qualified for the role. Since no one had ever seen his face, I chose the Lone Ranger, Clayton Moore."

The effectiveness of mural art relies to some degree on the theme of exaggerated contrast and extremes, and for mural artists this often means taking chances, jeopardizing the comfort of accepted conventions, and confronting what has not been done. Kent Twitchell, Terry Schoonhoven, John Wehrle and other superrealist mural artists embrace these concepts to create evocative works that stir our senses and beg for recognition. Each of us, having seen one of these murals, is left longing to see more.

Realist mural painter Tom Suriya evokes our powers of recognition and recall in a humorous and painterly manner. *You are the Star* (see page 120), a mural on the wall of an art deco commercial building in the heart of Hollywood, portrays an audience composed of movie stars gazing out at you — Marilyn Monroe, James Dean, Clark Gable, Charlie Chaplin, Marlon Brando — even E.T. As you look at this mural you, the viewer, become their center of attention. *You are the Star* is painted in an almost naive style that captures the likenesses of these favorite personalities and expresses a true affection for them, for their movies, and for days gone by.

"The response of countless individuals to my work has made it all worth the effort," Suriya says. "To see a smile on the face of someone viewing one of my murals has been my greatest reward."

The inclusion of numerous details and an affectionate attitude characterize many other murals throughout Los Angeles. Restaurants and other commercial buildings abound with murals, many anonymous, that celebrate life and utilize decorative painting techniques (see pages 16 and 44). Usually commissioned by the owner of a building or a resident business, these murals are often whimsical and light-hearted, and provide a charming change of pace that enlivens the neighborhood and entertains the viewer.

The Olympic murals on the freeways have a more dramatic effect (see page 119). Commissioned for the 1984 Olympics, sponsored by Cal Trans, California's Department of Highways, and designed and executed by accomplished mural artists, the Olympic murals are a tour de force of creative gusto and a visual embodiment of the lengths to which artists will go to express themselves and to make their art visible. Painted amid a jungle of freeways, clouds of sooty exhaust, and extremely precarious working conditions, the Olympic murals are a tribute to the vigorous expression of public art which exists in California and to the many accomplished artists who for years have been working in this genre.

"The wedding of public art and freeway walls in Los Angeles seemed like a marriage made in heaven," said Bob Goodell, Cal Trans Art Coordinator. "Using freeway walls for murals immediately expanded the viewing audience 1,000-fold — mostly delighting viewers, but occasionally infuriating them."

The brainchild of muralist Alonzo Davis, the Olympic murals were commissioned by the Los Angeles Olympic Organizing Committee and are meant to be seen from the fast lane as one enters downtown Los Angeles. Alonzo Davis and Kent Twitchell selected eight other muralists in addition to themselves to paint murals in a line from City Hall to the Coliseum for the 1984 Olympic Games. Each artist chosen had been creating murals for many years and had remained committed to the art form whether or not money was involved.

"The possibility of bringing together ten of the best public muralists in America on one project for an Olympic audience was beyond my wildest dreams," said Goodell.

The Olympic murals were an exhibition of street art by those who had developed the genre: Glenna Boltuch Avila, Judy Baca, Alonzo Davis, Willie Herrón, Frank Romero, Terry Schoonhoven, Roderick Sykes, Kent Twitchell, John Wehrle, and Richard Wyatt.

Creating the Olympic murals was an enormous undertaking and a sometimes harrowing experience for the artists. Each of the ten artists had to get permits from Cal Trans to begin work. Sketches were submitted for approval to the Los Angeles Olympic Organizing Committee, which financed the murals under the Los Angeles Olympics Art Fund (LAOAF).

To conform to safety standards set by Cal Trans, artists had to wear hard hats and vests and learn to use hand signals. Five of the artists had to erect concrete safety barriers at their own expense. Working hours were regulated, and work was not permitted during rush hour. Freeway sites were selected according to locations that were least distracting to the motorists and safest for the artists. In spite of all these precautions, one artist's pickup truck was hit by a car; another artist narrowly escaped injury when a palm tree near his mural caught fire.

Some of the mural walls stretched over 300 feet wide and up to 20 feet high — an enormous physical task to paint. The murals took more than a year to complete, and while they are an ever-present reminder of the 1984 Olympic Games, they also provide continuous visual excitement for motorists, and in their sheer monumentality and chutzpah represent the spirit of the city of Los Angeles.

The enormous scale of the Olympic murals, and the tremendous publicity surrounding their production, brought to the public an awareness of the processes through which public artworks can come into being, as well as an appreciation for the complexities of their production. The result of such public-access art activity is a growing public enthusiasm, and the art itself is a visible symbol of a commitment to the development of an urban aesthetic.

The benefits of an artistically enriched public environment are numerous and far-reaching. Murals, more than many other art forms, bring into focus the dynamics between artists and their communities. Whether they be "bandit" murals, done surreptitiously overnight on public walls without permission, or highly structured works of public art which take months of planning and elaborate financial structuring, these images affect us all.

We realized in creating this book that certain omissions would be unavoidable, and we knew that it would be an impossible task to include every mural we have seen. Some murals, because of their locations, were too difficult to photograph. Others disappeared or were painted over before we could return to photograph them. Many beautiful walls are not included here because their images cross the fine line between murals and graffiti, and that is another matter, another book entirely.

Our desire is to bring to you, the viewers and the readers of this book, a contemporary exhibit of this fascinating and enlightening wall art — multifaceted, larger-than-life images available for everyone to see and to enjoy. This book is a tribute to the vitality of mural art and to the many talented artists who are its creators.

— BETTY MERKEN

THE MURALS

Ed Ruscha Monument. Kent Twitchell, 1978-1987. Hill Street and Olympic Boulevard, Los Angeles.

"Ruscha reminded me of McQueen. Seven years after my first monument I selected Ruscha as a symbol of the L.A. art world. I had never met him — I sent him a note telling him what I wanted to do. He came to my studio in early 1978 for a photo session. I liked him very much and was glad my instincts had chosen him. We discussed L.A. and I found out that I share many of his feelings. I don't know of a better symbol for L.A. art.

"I painted his head in 1978 but I didn't like the results. A couple of years later I asked Ruscha to pose again. This time I carefully lit my subject as I have with every project since. The Ed Ruscha Monument *is actually Ruscha's head in 1980 and his body in 1978.*

"I had seen the wall and sketched it about two years before it was made available to me. It was just one of those magic walls anyone would like. Relatively on its own, not dwarfed by other structures, not minimized by ads all around it, and it was surrounded by flat, low parking lots, acres of cars to tower above.

"I want him to appear timeless, beyond fads or fashion . . . I had trouble with colors fading. I mixed colors from studying the baroque palette, warm glowing skin tones, etc. Within a year they would go cool, the yellows dropping out. I painted the new face one more time and again it cooled in a year. Now I'm using a very highly pigmented paint made for me in Australia."

— Kent Twitchell

13

El Corrido de Boyle Heights.
East Los Streetscapers, 1983. Soto
Street and Brooklyn Avenue, East
Los Angeles.

Brandelli's Brig. Arthur Mortimer,
1973. West Washington Boulevard,
Venice.

Ansel Adams Memorial.
Produced by the Gallery Scope
Mural Team: Jhu, Park, Song, G. Kim,
Bong, B. Kim, 1985. Highland
Avenue and Santa Monica Boulevard,
Los Angeles.

"*Living in an environment which is
filled with art can only create more
humanistic and artistic lives — lives
which include a sense that things
can be changed and profoundly
affected, and a sense that our lives
can create and achieve a positive
and cultural environment for the
next generations.*"

— Glenna Boltuch Avila
Former Director
City Wide Mural Project
Los Angeles

Untitled. Curtis Gutierrez, 1986.
Traction Avenue and Merrick Street,
Los Angeles. Commissioned by the
building owner to beautify artists'
lofts.

Magritte in Los Angeles. Noa Bornstein, 1984. Mike Miller's Chevron station, La Cienega Boulevard and Imperial Highway. Dedicated to the people of Los Angeles and to the spirit of Billy Gornel.

Inner City Relief. Richard Wyatt,
1982. Villa Gardens Artificial Kidney
Center, LaFayette Park Place and
Temple Street, Los Angeles.

Inyo-Crater. Donald Blumberg, 1984. Wilshire Boulevard and Sepulveda Boulevard, Los Angeles. Black and white original photographs laminated with various acrylic solutions.

21

Monument to Strother Martin.
Kent Twitchell, 1972. Kingsley and Fountain Avenue, Los Angeles.

"Strother was the best 'bad guy' I had ever seen. He fascinated me. Whenever I felt low I'd try to find a movie he was in. His small role would be worth the wait, he did it with such relish. Usually a John Ford or Sam Peckinpah movie was a good bet to include Strother. In Cool Hand Luke he was the prison warden who . . . recited the quote that characterized the times, 'What we have here is a failure to communicate.'

Strother heard I was painting him and he phoned me. We became friends and he used to call me regularly and practice lines to me just to get my reactions. He introduced me to several great character actors including Warren Oates, Denver Pyle, Jack Elam, L. Q. Jones. Strother was very dignified, very cultured."

— Kent Twitchell

Hector Street. Jane Golden, 1980.
Santa Monica Jewish Community
Center, 26th Street and Santa
Monica Boulevard, Santa Monica.

The Watchers. Kent Twitchell,
1984. Junior Arts Center, Barnsdall
Park, Los Angeles.

The Isle of California. Los Angeles Fine Arts Squad: Terry Schoonhoven, Vic Henderson, 1972 Butler Avenue near Santa Monica Boulevard, Los Angeles.

For early murals, longevity was not an issue. The paintings were treated as performances and allowed to disintegrate, as can be seen from these photos taken about 15 years apart.

Mom and Pop Farm Scene. J. Goley and S. Riley, 1982. Bev-Wood market storefront, Robertson Boulevard and Monte Mar Drive, Los Angeles.

Moe's Hardware Store. P. Astet, ca. 1985. 3044 Wabash Avenue, City Terrace, CA. Mural commissioned by owner to beautify building.

Neu's News Stand. KSN
Productions and WCA Gang, 1987.
Martel Avenue and Melrose Avenue,
Los Angeles. The newsstand owner
asked two different groups to paint
on this wall, the KSN group took the
right side of the door and the WCA
group took the space on the left.
Only cans of spray paint were used.

L. A. Freeway Kids. Glenna Boltuch Avila, 1984. Hollywood Freeway interchange at Los Angeles Street, Los Angeles. Sponsored by the Los Angeles Olympics Art Fund.

"What I wanted to do with this mural was to capture the spirit of the Olympics by painting the exuberant spirit of children."

— Glenna Boltuch Avila
Former Director
City Wide Mural Project
Los Angeles

Dial M. Bandit mural, artist and date unknown. Sunset Boulevard and Selma Avenue, Hollywood. Obscured by new building.

First Federal Savings. Artist and
date unknown. Ashland and Main
Street, Ocean Park.

Bertolt Brecht and Friends.
Frank A. Roys, 1982. Odyssey
Theater, Santa Monica Boulevard and
Bundy Drive, West Los Angeles.
Bertolt Brecht is shown playing the
flute in Munich at the Octoberfest.

Let the Dreams Begin. Artist
unknown, 1984. Figueroa
Apartments, King Boulevard and
Figueroa Street, Los Angeles.

Ghosts of the Barrio. Wayne Healy, 1974. Ramona Gardens Housing Project, Lancaster Avenue and Evergreen Avenue, Lincoln Heights, Los Angeles.

De Adelita. Carlos Almaraz, 1976. Ramona Gardens Housing Project, Lancaster Avenue and Evergreen Avenue, Lincoln Heights, Los Angeles.

Untitled. Artist and date unknown. Ramona Gardens Housing Project, Lancaster Avenue and Evergreen Avenue, Lincoln Heights, Los Angeles.

Untitled. Artist and date unknown. Ramona Gardens Housing Project, Lancaster Avenue and Evergreen Avenue, Lincoln Heights, Los Angeles.

Untitled. Judith Hernandez, 1976. Ramona Gardens Housing Project, Lancaster Avenue and Evergreen Avenue, Lincoln Heights, Los Angeles.

Six L.A. Artists. Kent Twitchell, 1979. Employment Development Department Building, Engracia Avenue, Torrance.

"This was the second monument to visual artists. These six, left to right, Marta Chaffee, Alonzo Davis, Paul Czirban, Oliver Nowlin, Eloy Torrez and Waynna Kato, all graduated at various times from Otis Art Institute in Los Angeles. The wall was a competition sponsored by the Office of the State Architect of the California Arts Council. The wall is the east side of the unemployment building in Torrance, California. I thought it particularly appropriate to paint artists on an unemployment building."

— Kent Twitchell

37

Changes. Tom Suriya, 1984. Yawl Alley, Venice. The transformation of the Venice beach community is depicted in this mural painted on a garage door.

Château des Chats, Aaron,
1979. 2817 Clearwater Street, Los
Angeles.

Reflection. Roderick Sykes, 1984. Harbor Freeway Flower Street on-ramp. Sponsored by the Los Angeles Olympics Art Fund.

Pyramid Mural #2. Alonzo Davis,
1987. La Brea Avenue near Coliseum
Avenue, Los Angeles. Sponsored by
Brockman Gallery.

Unfinished Canvas. Michael Kelly,
1985. Beverly Boulevard and LaPeer
Drive, Los Angeles.

An Italian Street Scene. Susan
Brabeau, 1983-1984. Miceli's
Restaurant, Cahuenga Boulevard
West and Regal Street, North
Hollywood.

"To me, art is an unending search
for new ways to express myself. If
one would follow the life histories of
the world's great painters, they
would find that most masters start
with an objective to reproduce what
they see, but it's almost inevitable
that their objectives grow into what
and how they feel and why they feel
it.

"When I first felt such emotional
involvement I realized I had finally
found my rock, my self, in that
murky haze out there. And the best
part is that it doesn't breed
contentment . . . but unlimited, clear
flight into the unknown."

— Susan Brabeau

"I get the biggest kick seeing someone try to use a door that I just painted on a wall. That's when I know that I've fulfilled my artistic choice."

— Susan Brabeau

City Scape. Terry Schoonhoven, 1984. Sixth Street bypass of the Harbor Freeway, Los Angeles. Sponsored by the Los Angeles Olympics Art Fund.

Homage to John Outterbridge.
Alonzo Davis, 1980. Watts Towers
Arts Center, East 107th Street,
Watts, Los Angeles.

"As a painter/muralist I am
motivated to reach audiences
indifferent to galleries and museums
who respond to and get excited by
seeing art in public places. My
motivation comes from a desire to
share, the excitement of working
large, and a concern that art should
be for everyone."

— Alonzo Davis

Peace and Love. Elliott Pinkney,
1976. Watts Towers Arts Center,
East 107th Street, Watts, Los
Angeles.

Shyaam. Khylo, 1984. Midcity
Auto Body Shop, Gage Avenue and
Western Avenue, Los Angeles.

Chinese Celestial Dragon. Fu-Ding Cheng, 1986. Gin Ling Way (between Hill Street and Broadway) in Chinatown, Los Angeles. Fu-Ding had seen this mural as a boy and has restored it twice in the last 20 years.

A & M Recording Studio. P.
Prince and M. Cotton, 1979. La Brea
Avenue near Sunset Boulevard,
Hollywood.

Return of the Maya. John Valadez, 1979. 3400 block North Figueroa Street, Highland Park, Los Angeles. Sponsored by the City Wide Mural Project.

Return of the Maya.

Niño y Caballo. Frank Romero, 1984. Victor Clothing Company, Broadway near Third Street, Los Angeles.

"Niño y Caballo . . . is a simple allegory of freedom. It is about an experience the owner of Victor Clothing Company, Paul Harter, had in Mexico. There he saw a young boy riding on a horse with such joy and abandon that he never forgot the sight. I liked his story so much I did the painting from it."

— Frank Romero

"You're not only taking in the mural, but also all of the surrounding landscape. Its location becomes important."

— Fiona Whitney
Turske & Whitney Gallery
Los Angeles

El Nuevo Fuego. East Los Streetscapers, 1984. Victor Clothing Company, Broadway near Second Street, Los Angeles.

The Pope of Broadway. Eloy Torres, 1984. The Victor Clothing Company Building, Third Street near Broadway, Los Angeles.

Evergreen Painting Company.
Fronk, Hetzel, Monson, and
Vanderwell, undated. Fourth Street
and Hill Street, Los Angeles.

57

Untitled. Wes Hall and Paul Nash, 1975-1977. Compton High School Gym, 601 South Acacia, Compton. Friends, students, and community members collaborated on this mural.

Untitled. R. E. Cirerol, 1976. Bonnie Beach Place and Olympic Boulevard, East Los Angeles.

Black Folk Art in America Exhibition. Glenna Boltuch Avila and others, 1983. Painted on the back wall of the Craft and Folk Art Museum, 5814 Wilshire Boulevard, Los Angeles, in conjunction with an exhibition of Black folk art. Painted by Glenna, four other artists, and 65 elementary school children.

"The children's interpretations of the Black Folk Art in America exhibition were at the same time innocent and sophisticated. The children attempted to recreate the same innocence and spirit of the folk art on exhibit on the outside wall of the museum."

— Glenna Boltuch Avila
Former Director
City Wide Mural Project
Los Angeles

St. Charles Painting. Los Angeles
Fine Arts Squad: Terry Schoonhoven
and Vic Henderson, 1979. Windward
Avenue and Speedway, Venice.

The Freeway Lady. Kent Twitchell, 1974. Hollywood Freeway near Alvarado exit, Los Angeles. Sponsored by the Inner City Mural Project.

Actress Lillian Bronson posed as the Freeway Lady. Twitchell wanted this piece to serve as a monument to old people, and it has become his most widely accepted mural.

Untitled. Roland Welton, 1984.
5100 Crenshaw Boulevard, Los
Angeles. Sponsored by Brockman
Gallery.

Untitled. James Borders, 1984.
5100 Crenshaw Boulevard, Los
Angeles. Sponsored by Brockman
Gallery.

Untitled. Roland Welton, 1984.
5100 Crenshaw Boulevard, Los
Angeles. Sponsored by Brockman
Gallery.

Hollywood Sunset. Dino Schofield and Jeanne Romano, 1980. Theatrecraft Playhouse, Gardner Street and Sunset Boulevard, Los Angeles.

Steve McQueen Monument.
Kent Twitchell, 1971. Union Avenue and 12th Avenue, Los Angeles.

"I cast McQueen as Moses, his eyes white, after talking to God."

"I never met him. I painted him from photos in magazines and a poster I saw. His son Chad said McQueen saw the mural in the middle of the night while he was driving his pickup around L.A., something he did to unwind. He didn't even know where. He woke Chad up to tell him about it."

— Kent Twitchell

Dancing Figures. Artist and date unknown. Near First Street Bridge at Utah Street, Los Angeles.

The Original Home of Simon Rodia. Richard Haro, 1975. East 107th Street, Watts, Los Angeles.

As a child, Haro watched the towers being built and later was asked to do this mural.

Hog Heaven. Les Grimes and
Arno Jordan. Begun in 1957. Farmer
John Processing Plant, Soto Street
and Bandini Avenue, Los Angeles.

Untitled. Alonzo Davis, 1982.
Painted on the side of Davis's studio,
4330 Degnan Avenue, Crenshaw
Boulevard near 43rd Street, Los
Angeles. Sponsored by Brockman
Gallery.

Reruns. Kent Twitchell, 1981. 2166
West Sunset Boulevard, Los Angeles.

Roses of the Rose. René Holovsky and Renate Greene, 1979-1980. Rose Cafe, Rose Avenue and Hampton, Ocean Park.

Intrinsic. Gray, 1986. Bandit mural. Mateo Avenue and Santa Fe Avenue, Los Angeles.

NaNa. Eric Leach and Kirk Canning, 1985. Broadway near Second Street, Santa Monica. Painted with spray cans by two employees of the store.

"Street art is no different than fine art. With street art you choose your viewing crowd through location and there is no red tape. It is an exclusive showing; your work is not lost or pushed aside . . . Art is for all eyes, not just those of rich intellectuals."

— Kirk Canning, a.k.a. "KIZ"

Galileo, Apollo, Jupiter. John
Wehrle, 1983-1984. Santa Ana
Freeway between Broadway and
Spring Street. Sponsored by the Los
Angeles Olympics Art Fund.

Legends of Hollywood. Eloy
Torres, 1983. Sunset Boulevard and
Hudson Street, Hollywood.

Eyes. Ruben Brucelyn and Kent Twitchell, 1986-1987. Glendale Boulevard and Sunset Boulevard underpass.

"I think some people must be very excited . . . viewing the murals from the freeway at 55 m.p.h., and others have little or no reaction. The excited people, however, see a little more each time they drive by, and quite soon they want to find another mural to look at, and it becomes an adventure to drive around looking for paintings on the sides of buildings, in tunnels . . . and one hopes that some of these people will venture out of their cars and into museums and galleries to spend more time looking at art."

— Fiona Whitney, Director
Turske & Whitney Gallery
Los Angeles

Untitled, unfinished. James Borders, 1985. 52nd Street and Crenshaw Boulevard, Los Angeles. Sponsored by Brockman Gallery.

Casa Carnitas. Artist and date unknown. On the side of a restaurant of the same name, Beverly Boulevard and Kenmore Avenue, Los Angeles.

Untitled. Artist unknown, 1978.
Estrada Court Housing Project,
Granda Vista Avenue and Olympic
Boulevard, East Los Angeles.

Unbridled. David S. Gordon, 1986.
Fourth Street and Ocean Park
Boulevard. Santa Monica. Sponsored
by the Frederick Weisman
Foundation of Art.

Nearly a block long, this mural
depicts a dozen or more carousel
horses unbridling themselves and
breaking away from the landmark
Santa Monica Pier Carousel.

Unbridled (continued).

"The production of public art must balance the influences of the artist and the community in which it exists. Otherwise it doesn't belong."
— David Gordon

Unbridled (continued).

Ocean Park Pier. Jane Golden, 1976. Ocean Park Boulevard and Main Street, Santa Monica. Sponsored by the City Wide Mural Project.

Two Blue Whales. Margaret Garcia, Randy Geraldi, 1978. Beethoven Street and Venice Boulevard, Los Angeles.

Sports Mural. Ruben Brucelyn, 1984. Painted over the untitled mural at left.

Untitled. Eugene Greenland, Ray Vanderhagen, Leonard Castellanos, Gerry Cabazos, and Tomas Gonzales, 1973. Glendale Boulevard, Echo Park (across from Echo Park Lake), Los Angeles. Sponsored by the Mechicano Art Center.

This mural was painted to replace a graffiti-covered staircase in 1973. The mural itself was replaced eleven years later by Brucelyn's *Sports Mural.*

La Familia. Los Dos Streetscapers: W. Healy and D. Botello, 1977. North Broadway and Daly, Lincoln Heights, Los Angeles.

"People identify with the murals because murals tell the history of the people themselves. They see their lives reflected in the murals on a heroic scale. Those muralists who set themselves a goal of bringing pride to the people have often consciously encouraged this tendency to identify . . . Murals thus become a vehicle for a process of self-definition by the people."

— Glenna Boltuch Avila
Former Director
City Wide Mural Project
Los Angeles

La Reina de Los Angeles de Poruincula. Joe Gonzalez, 1984. Vermont Avenue and Leighton Avenue, Los Angeles. Sponsored by the Los Angeles Olympic Organizing Committee Youth Art Program.

Fall of Icarus. John Wehrle, 1978.
Market Street and Speedway
Avenue, Venice.

Untitled. Artist and date unknown. Third Street near the Long Beach Freeway, Los Angeles.

Sunset Junction Street Fair. Carlos Callejo and Louis Jacinto, 1982. Sunset Boulevard and Lucile Avenue, Los Angeles. Sponsored by the City Wide Mural Project.

Bride and Groom. Kent Twitchell, 1975. Victor Clothing Company, Broadway near Third Street, Los Angeles.

"The murals seem to make a very powerful statement to me, which is: Man/Woman is capable of so much."
— Fiona Whitney, Director
   Turske & Whitney Gallery
   Los Angeles

© 1982 Flying Colors S.F.

RESERVED
PARKING
ONLY

Joslyn Park. Arthur Mortimer, 1981. Beverly Avenue and Kensington Road, Santa Monica. Dedicated to Valerie Nordstrom Barnard.

Spago Restaurant. Flying Colors, 1982. Horn Avenue and Sunset Boulevard, Los Angeles.

Untitled. James Avila, 1985. Whittier Boulevard and Bradshowe Avenue, East Los Angeles. Commissioned by owner to protect the building from graffiti.

Two Ways. Daniel Martinez, Playboy Gang, 1985. Pico Boulevard and Fedora Street, Los Angeles. Sponsored by Community Youth Gang Services.

"I got involved in 1969. I was tired of looking at graffiti and decided to paint over it. I used to do graffiti on the walls myself, so now I am giving back to the community through my murals what I used to take away from it. I'm still expressing myself on the wall and I am leaving a legacy for my children."

— Daniel Martinez

Mother and Child. Curry, 1982. Evergreen Community School, Florence Avenue and Normandie Avenue, Los Angeles.

Untitled. A. S. Bloomfield, 1981. Apartment house, Seventh Street and Pier Avenue, Santa Monica.

French Water Colors, James Paul Brown, 1982-1983. Ocean Park Boulevard and Barnard Avenue, Venice.

Fairfax Community Mural. A.
Mortimer, S. Anaya, P. Fleischman,
1985. Oakwood Avenue and
Fairfax Avenue, Los Angeles.

*"To me, murals are a way of
bringing something of aesthetic
value into a community or
neighborhood. I want my pieces to
add something to a neighborhood,
and to perhaps stimulate thinking or
appreciation for one's surroundings
in a new way."*
— Arthur Mortimer

Warriors Yesterday and Today.
Daniel Martinez, 1986. In memory
of Chico Barrera, for the East Los
Angeles 13 Gang. Brooklyn Avenue
and Fickett Street, East Los Angeles.
Sponsored by Community Youth
Gang Services.

James. Richard Wyatt, 1983.
Harbor Freeway at Adams Street
Bridge, Los Angeles. Sponsored by
the Los Angeles Olympics Art Fund.

Jesus. Kent Twitchell, assisted by the Solo Gang, 1984. 111th Street and Vermont Avenue, South Central Los Angeles.

"I consider myself a regionalist religious folk artist. My murals are similar in some ways to dramatic productions. . . .

"In 1984, I was contacted by Solo Gang leaders from South L.A. They wanted a painting of Jesus on an exterior wall in their barrio. Bob Goodell, art director for Cal Trans [California Department of Transportation] put me together with Father Dennis Berry of the Church of the Ascension, who served the barrio near 111th Street and Vermont.

"There had been several murders in the area. In fact, the day Father Dennis drove me to see the wall, I was introduced to a boy the priest had been helping. He spoke highly of him, of how well he was doing now, after so much difficulty in his youth. A few hours later he was dead, his throat cut.

"We painted the Jesus on the south wall of the Tiger Liquor Store. The wall was riddled with bullets. We worked every Saturday through the summer. Hispanics of all ages helped paint as well as gang members, blacks, Anglos.

"After it was finished, the community and Ascension Church put tables filled with food in front of Jesus' open arms and dedicated the mural to the people. The gang protects the mural to this day."

— Kent Twitchell

John Muir Woods. Jane Golden,
1978. Ocean Park Boulevard and
Lincoln Boulevard, Santa Monica.
Sponsored by CEDA.

Los Angeles Produce Market.
Tom Suriya, 1986. On the produce
market, Eighth Street and Central
Avenue, Los Angeles.

California's Finest. Tom Suriya,
1986. Eighth Street and Central
Avenue, Los Angeles.

Wall of Fame. Tom Suriya, 1984.
KFAC Building, Yucca Street and
McCadden Place, Hollywood.

Respect What You See. Bill
Butler, 1979. Gage Avenue and
Brooklyn Avenue, Boyle Heights, Los
Angeles.

Venice Medical Building. Joe Bravo, 1976. Pacific Avenue and Market Street, Venice.

Untitled. Glenna Boltuch Avila and the Watts Towers Arts Center teenagers, 1979. Watts Tower Arts Center, East 107th Street, Watts, Los Angeles.

112

Dream of Flight. David Botello, 1973–1976. Estrada Courts Housing Project, Lorena Avenue and Olympic Boulevard, Los Angeles.

"Murals are about people having an effect on their cities, for taking responsibility for their visual and physical environment, leaving records of their lives and concerns, and in the process transforming neighborhoods, reducing vandalism and graffiti and creating new artists out of the youth of our communities."
— Glenna Boltuch Avila
Former Director
City Wide Mural Project
Los Angeles

Moonscapes. Los Dos
Streetscapers, 1979. Department of
Motor Vehicles Building, West
Washington Boulevard and Purdue
Avenue, Culver City.

Aztec Warrior. Edela Loza, 1978.
Alameda Theatre, Whittier
Boulevard and Woods Avenue, East
Los Angeles.

Counterclockwise from left:

Untitled. The Clayton 14 Gang, 1984. Melrose Avenue and Heliotrope Street. Mostly painted out by early 1987.

Untitled. Artist and date unknown. Union Avenue and 11th Place, Los Angeles.

In Memories to the Guerrivero Heroico. Terero, 1978. Estrada Court Housing Project, Grande Vista Avenue and Olympic Boulevard, Los Angeles.

Clockwise from right:

Untitled. Artist and date unknown. Ramona Gardens Housing Project, Lancaster Avenue and Evergreen Avenue, Lincoln Heights, Los Angeles.

Untitled. James Borders, 1984. 5100 Crenshaw Boulevard, Los Angeles. Sponsored by Brockman Gallery.

Untitled. James Borders, 1984. 5100 Crenshaw Boulevard, Los Angeles. Sponsored by Brockman Gallery.

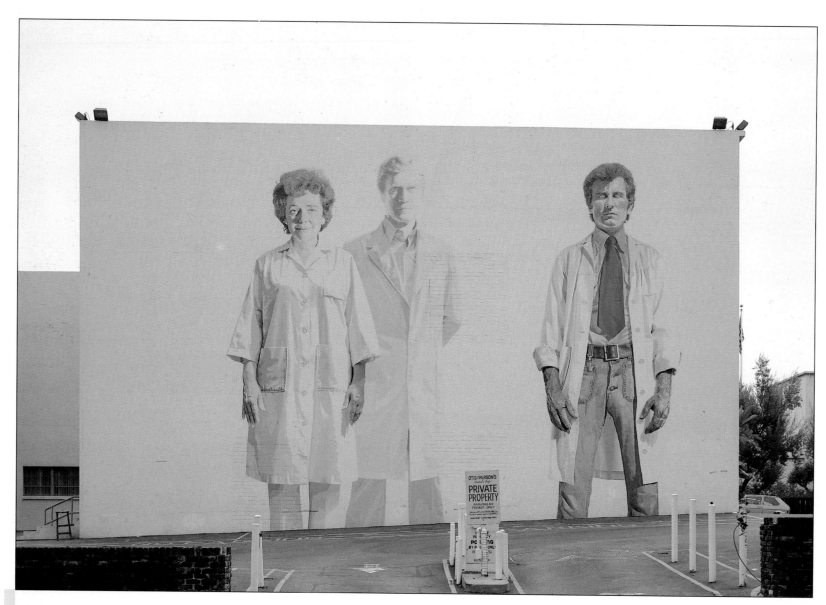

**The Holy Trinity with the
Virgin.** Kent Twitchell, 1977-1978.
The Otis Art Institute of Parsons
School of Design in Los Angeles,
Wilshire Boulevard and Carondelet.

Going to the Olympics. Frank Romero, 1983-1984. Hollywood Freeway near Los Angeles Street, Los Angeles. Sponsored by the Los Angeles Olympics Art Fund.

"Going to the Olympics, *the Olympic freeway mural, was based on the banners used in the processions along the roads leading to the original Olympic games in Greece. The murals along the freeway are a contemporary reference to these banners. The five automobiles with hearts floating above them are symbolic of Los Angeles and its welcome to the citizens of five continents participating in the games.*"
— Frank Romero

You are the Star. Tom Suriya, 1983. Wilcox and Hollywood Boulevard, Los Angeles.

Untitled. Campeo & Barrena. Date
unknown. Seventh Street and Wall
Street, Los Angeles.

Remembrances of Yesterday — Dreams of Tomorrow. Judith Hernandez, 1982. Arcadia Street and Spring Street, Los Angeles.

In the Style of Patrick Nagel. Bandit mural, artist unknown. Ca. 1985. Sepulveda Boulevard near Sunset Boulevard, Los Angeles.

Untitled. Artist and date unknown. Westmoreland Street and Beverly Boulevard, Los Angeles.

Willowbrook Mural Project.
Richard Wyatt, 1979-1980.
Wilmington Avenue and El Segundo
Boulevard, Compton, CA.
Willowbrook Junior High School.

*"The scale of the city . . . is low,
flat . . . its profile complements
murals. Also the good weather
makes it possible to have artists
working outside all year 'round."*
— Fiona Whitney, Director
Turske & Whitney Gallery
Los Angeles

Mary: 7th Street Altarpiece.
Kent Twitchell, 1983–1984. Portrait
of artist Lita Albuquerque as a
contemporary Madonna. Seventh
Street underpass of the Harbor
Freeway, Los Angeles.

INDEX